Paperback ISBN: 979-8-9905993-0-7

First paperback edition May 2024
Publisher: *Dark Lunar Nyad Press*

NyaSAbernathy.com

WELCOME,
WONDER

"Sheesh. I was already familiar with Nya's work and writing style, but I was completely taken by surprise at how much *Welcome, Wonder* would resonate with me. In her beautiful way of calling in her readers, she uses a format of: Question, Affirmation, and Noticing. In one of the entries, Nya recalls a moment in a university quad where a moment with a telescope caused a visceral reaction. Her question then asks about a time when the reader had a reaction to wonder. I immediately was transported to an experience I had with a family of deer that brought me to instantaneous 'tearful joy.'

In another entry, Nya describes a moment on a beach. As I am reading this particular entry, I was literally and physically jolted. While reading *Welcome, Wonder*, I realized that not only is the book *for* me, this book is *about* me. And I truly believe that this book is about all of you, too. Take some time to delve deep into yourself, your thoughts, and your beliefs. Make time for wonder. You deserve this book."

-Courtney Cook, speaker and author of *WORTHY! A book for kids of all ages*

"In a time of relentless catastrophe, stepping into wonder seems almost impossible. This invitation is not one of escapism but of connection with wonder as our teacher. *Welcome, Wonder* offers an opportunity for sacred exploration that will ground you in your humanity while making room for revelation in wonderment with Nya Abernathy as your trustworthy guide. May you be filled with holy anticipation as you welcome wonder."

-Rebekah James Lovett, writer and founder of Thambusami

"I have long been an admirer of Nya's writing. Her ability to communicate curiosity, wonder, awe, and childlikeness is infectious. This book truly does not disappoint and communicates these elements in ways that are lifegiving, clear, and affirming of human dignity. I recommend this book to all who are feeling weary, burned out, or just craving something inspiring."

-Robert Monson, writer at *Musings From A Broken Heart* and co-director at Enfleshed

"*Welcome, Wonder* takes us beyond what we fully know or can possibly hold while affirming our divinity and holding us in belovedness. We may stumble back before the 'awe-filled' as we greet the limits of our humanity and discover more questions than answers. On a journey such as this, it is helpful to have a guide who is patient, passionate, and empathetic as we let ourselves come close. Nya frequents the wilderness of wonder herself, as a lover of the stars, and as one who writes with devoted knowledge and openness. Her curiosity is as contagious as the ethic of care laced throughout each prompt. This book is a gift to those seeking to awaken to both ordinary and extraordinary wonders alongside spiritually expansive practices."

-Rose J. Percy, M.Div, theologian and writer at *A Gentle Landing*

"A wonderful book to help us process our stories, our goodness, the light that all of us possess. *Welcome, Wonder* is accessible, positive, and life giving. You'll likely find elements of yourself that you didn't know existed or become reacquainted with parts of your story you've missed or buried."

-Matthew Paul Turner, author of *You Will Always Belong* and *When God Made You*

"Nya has an uncanny ability to draw her kin into the same experience of absolute joy and wonder. We've needed and many of us have been waiting for a voice like hers. Her passion for the cosmic story that is being told by the universe is infectious. I consider her one of my guides into and through the mysteries of the divine."

-Tamice Spencer-Helms, founder of Sub:Culture, Inc. and author of *Faith Unleavened: The Wilderness Between Trayvon Martin and George Floyd*

"'Indifference to the sublime wonder of living is the root of sin,'" wrote American mystic, prophet, and rabbi, Abraham Joshua Heschel. Nya Abernathy shares Heschel's 'radical amazement' at the sheer givenness of this moment, this cosmos, this life. More than that, Nya, like a loving friend, a kind aunt, and a wise spiritual director, is inviting you to embrace the gift of your own life and relax into being your wonder-full self."

-Jarrod McKenna, Australian peace award winning nonviolence educator, activist, pastor and co-founder of gazaceasefirepilgrimage.com

"After soaking up Nya Abernathy's gorgeous writing for a few years now, I think of her every single time I hear the word 'wonder' (okay, and 'stars' and 'space' and 'the cosmos' too). Her passion for—and obsession with—wonder makes me want more of it in my life. And now, with her book, *Welcome, Wonder*, I've gotten my wish. Short, beautiful reflections to start my day with what I hope will become a lifelong habit: more noticing, more affirmation, more wonder."

—Marla Taviano, author of *unbelieve*, *jaded*, and *whole*

"If you are looking for expansion in your life, if you are looking to take up space, figuratively and literally, then you MUST allow the WONDER of this book to find a place in your quiet time. Whatever you wish to call it, whatever time you seek to set aside where you meet with yourself and go about the business of just BEING your full-of-wonder self, then allow Nya to be your wonder teacher and follow along with her as she gently and graciously guides you to that deeper knowing inside of you that is inviting you into what you were created and meant to be... a part of it all. Do you know how BIG that is? With some help from all the planets and elements in all the galaxies (including and especially our very own feelings), and through the awe-inspiring voice of a star-gazing dreamer, Nya has set the stage for you to step into the center of the universe where you will find yourself, the Eternal, and the world wide web of everything: you and me, the micro and the macro and all that lies in between and beyond."

-Tina Strawn, owner of Legacy Trips and author of *Are We Free Yet? The Black, Queer Guide To Divorcing America*

"Nya Abernathy lures us beyond modernity's mechanistic lens of our world to behold the cosmos with eyes and hearts wide open. In *Welcome, Wonder*, content and form align, as her prose moves across the page and gestures you into deeper awe, expansiveness, and belonging in creation. Drawn from the lived experience of someone who rediscovered the mystery of life and found delight in her journey, these daily mindfulness reflections are our needed training wheels into the practice of wonder. I highly recommend reading this with a journal in hand, and with gathered friends, for lively discussion around this lovely book!"

-Drew G. I. Hart, associate professor of Theology at Messiah University and author of *Who Will Be A Witness?: Igniting Activism for God's Justice, Love, and Deliverance*

"You need this book. Why? To slow down the harried pace of life and distractions, to breathe deep the wonder of presence, and to reorient yourself to actually see and experience the miraculous that exists all around (and within) you. There is so much wonder in the world to rediscover and reconnect with. Engaging in wonder makes us more ourselves—more attuned with our senses, souls, and minds to the world beyond the blue light of our devices. Nya's book gives us back our inheritance of wonder and allows us to claim it with thought-provoking examples, empowering affirmations, and insightful questions."

-Sharifa Stevens, co-author: *Only Light Can Do That: 60 Days of MLK - Devotions for Kids*; contributor: *Vindicating the Vixens: Revisiting Sexualized, Vilified, and Marginalized Women of the Bible*

"Reading *Welcome, Wonder* brings tears to my eyes as I am moved by the heartfelt invitations to root into our shared humanity and the Earth. Nya's insightful and reflective observations shed light on the ways we've been fragmented and separated from our connections with each other and the land. It's a poignant call to action, urging us to mend those broken ties and rediscover the joy of genuine human connection.

Welcome, Wonder is a masterpiece that has the power to transform lives. It's not just a book; it's a guide, a mentor, and a source of inspiration. As we navigate the pages, we find ourselves invited to embrace a world of awe and wonder, fostering a profound sense of connection with ourselves, others, and the world around us."

- Tommy (Allgood) Garvin, The Allgood Collective

ACKNOWLEDGEMENTS

In the following pages you'll find the names of many who have been a key part in this book being conceived, gestating, and birthed. Of course there are even more.

I could write an entirely separate book of just acknowledgements for those who have been alongside me in wonder and awe and writing. I won't. I deeply honor each one who has honored me with Love and care and encouragement.

I desire to specifically thank Marla Taviano. I am so glad you "made me write this book." Thank you, friend, for your support, encouragement, and loads of Love.

DEDICATION

To Myron,
who told me it'd been too long since
I'd hung out with The Stars.

This book is a result of your
Love, care, and deep knowledge of me.

Thank you.
I Love you.

CONTENTS

Foreword

I move through the world as a preacher, a pastor, and sometimes a prophet. People come to me with expectations that I will make sense of the world, their lives, the Bible, and God. In almost a decade of ministry, two decades of being a mother, and a lifetime in a Black female body, it has been a journey to accept that I do not have all of the answers. I've had to accept that some things just don't make sense. In many situations, when folks come to me in pain and full of grief, there is no "right answer."

When I began to lean into a posture of curiosity instead of a search for certainty, my faith became deeper, wider, and more expansive. Curiosity activated a holy imagination that brought the Bible to life in previously unseen ways. Curiosity opened the door to theologies that gave me new perspectives and more exciting questions. Curiosity allows me to sit with mystery, unknowns, and miracles with gratitude and expectation. Part of my work is to help people see that questions can unlock new realities.

I felt the whispers of new realities when I read *Welcome, Wonder*. Something settled in my soul when I read those words - *Welcome, Wonder*. Nya's words, invitations, and questions touched a longing that I hadn't noticed in the busyness of life. I found myself repeating "welcome, wonder" with a deep breath and gentle smile. Wonder feels like an invitation to rest, notice, and allow wisdom to unfurl at its own pace. Like any good host, I realized that if I genuinely wanted to welcome wonder, I would need to prepare a space in my heart, mind, soul, and body. Some of us know what it feels like to be "welcomed" to a space that is not ready for you. This book will help you to make space for wonder in your life.

I met Nya while leading a cohort for Black Women and nonbinary folks with the organization Liberated Together. It was a sacred space grounded in the invitation to simply be. In a world full of demands, reactivity, and to-do lists, it was a gift to hold space for my sisters and siblings. During our time together, we reconnected with ourselves and each other through lament, intentional rest, and joy. I watched jaws unclench, shoulders settle, and lungs expand with fresh breaths of freedom. I laughed until my stomach hurt when Nya pulled out the case of her golden microphone for our show and tell.

Our relationship has deepened through sweet and deep conversations, voice memos that make me cackle in the middle of the night, and a steady presence of love, support, and celebration.

Because of Nya, I see the sky differently. Because of Nya, I'm more aware of the Spirit that connects us to each other and to the universe. I trust her to hold me on the journey of wonder that weaves together faith, stars, physics, and my body and soul.

Welcome, Wonder is a guide on becoming a good host to wonder in your life. I'm grateful to be on this journey with you.

Rev. Riana Shaw Robinson
Birthing Pastor, Miriam's Song Church

Introduction

If our religion is based on salvation, our chief emotions will be fear and trembling. If our religion is based on wonder, our chief emotion will be gratitude.

Carl Jung

Wonder saved me. I mean that.

In 2021, I was burnt out on seeking peace during a pandemic, and, with young kids (including my young start-up), my heart was weary and terrified. What would this world become? How could I make it better? Something was missing, but I didn't know what.

My husband pointed me back to a place of joy I hadn't visited in a long time: space. Well, I haven't been to outer space. He was referring to the television shows I used to watch, like *How The Universe Works*, that would spark awe in me.

I had forgotten.

So, one night, exhausted and feeling useless in the world, I got in bed early, turned out all the lights, and let filmmakers, artists, and scientists dump wonder into my soul. It was medicine. It was magic. It stoked my imagination in ways I'd left unattended. Suddenly, I wanted to write so many things about all the wonder and beauty. I was introduced to some extraordinary scientists (I have a few favorite astrophysicists because, yes, I'm *that* nerdy). It led me to devour books—mostly audiobooks—about the Earth and the cosmos, what we've learned, and the stories we've told.

In 2022 I started curating my wonder writing in my Substack publication, "Of Earth & Of Stars," where I explore wonder and awe in the context of spirituality and the cosmos. This monthly offering came into the world with so much support from my husband Myron, Marla Taviano, and Erin Wang, among others.

This book is a result of my transformative journey with wonder. This book is my invitation to you to be in conversation with me—and anyone else you read this book with—about awe and opening yourself up to it. Wonder is vast because it's everywhere. You can move through your life seeing wonder in places you haven't seen it before. It just takes some practice. This book is a guide for your practice.

Notes on language:
While this book is not religious or specifically faith-based, wonder is deeply spiritual. That comes out in more obvious ways through some phrasing you will see. This includes "The Eternal"—an expansive term

for God I use often—as well as some references to the story of Jesus of Nazareth from The Holy Bible.

When you see me capitalizing the "L" on the word Love, it's meaningful to note I first saw this differentiation from Deidra Riggs[1]. Its purpose is to indicate that I am not employing a general, colloquial use of the word "love." Capitalized Love is the energy that created and animates the cosmos. Capitalized Love is the entity that imprints its fingerprints on everything—including you and me. Capitalized Love is a specific, creative, wonder-filled Love we can share between us because we are formed of it; there's just so much that aids our forgetting this. Writing capital-L-Love is a way I choose to practice remembering. If it speaks to you, feel free to use it as well.

Instead of saying "non-human" or "other-than-human" when referring to entities and creation that aren't human, I'm picking up the phrase "more-than-human." I first read this phrase in *Nature-Based Therapy* by Dr. Nevin J. Harper, Kathryn Rose, and David Segal. When I heard it again in conversation with my dear friend and colleague, Samantha E. Lioi, we discussed this phrase as an expansive callback to Indigenous worldviews influencing our ways of being: the reciprocity and interdependence of creation as a whole, in which humans are neither the pinnacle nor the center but a significant and interwoven part.

These are reference points for me because of my own formation and spirituality. I offer them to you with openness. May they meet you right where you are. May you hear what you need with comfort and connection.

About the format:

If you went through one entry a day from start to finish, you would finish the book in three lunar cycles—or one season. If you are really into this idea, you can start on a solstice, an equinox, a full moon, or a new moon. Also, you can start whenever you'd like.

The book is broken up into three cycles with twenty-eight entries each. Each entry has four sections with space included for you to write or doodle as part of your wonder practice. You can do all four each time you come to these pages or pick one or two sections to engage. Each season of life feels different, and we feel different in it. If, in this season, all you need is a daily affirmation, I gotchu. Engage the affirmations this season. Return to the book next season to see what you have space for.

Bottom line: Go through the book at whatever pace and level of engagement works for you. I'm grateful you are here.

As I welcome you, feel free to speak this simple yet profound intention as we begin and throughout the journey:
Welcome, Wonder.

First Cycle

"All of the things we cherish in this world were made inside the bellies of stars."

Aomawa Shields, PhD
Life On Other Planets: A Memoir of Finding My Place in the Universe

"Essentially, we are beings of energy
and light in a universe that emits both."

Dr. Barbara A. Holmes
Race and the Cosmos, 2nd Ed.

Offering

There are big inducers of wonder. Babies being born, the kindness of entire communities toward the suffering, seeing the aurora borealis with your own eyes, Indigenous languages being resurrected by descendants of those who once spoke them freely. These are obvious awe-producers. But you don't have to wait for the big productions to welcome wonder. You can find wonder waiting for you in your breath—for your breath is proof of your here-ness, your belonging, our inherent connection. Wonder is with you as you take in the everyday stimuli of the world alive around you. Wonder woos with a slight facial expression, the texture of a fabric, imagining beyond imposed boundaries, and in being known and Loved. Wonder is here, ready to be welcomed by you.

Question:

Where is it easy for you to freely greet wonder?

Affirmation:

I am in tune with the everyday wonder around me.

Noticing:

What are you noticing today about not being aware of wonder?

Offering

Why are we obsessed with light when most of creation is dark? Think about the depths of the ocean. Consider the understory of the forest and contemplate humus. Reflect on what happens inside of your body, which is mostly encased in darkness. Life itself forms in the dark. The darkness of a womb. The darkness of a seed in the ground. When we turn our heads away from our terrain out to the cosmos, 95% of the known universe is dark[2]. And yet, light is what we gravitate toward. Is it really just because it helps us see, or is there something else about dark that makes many of us claw for light? Are we so divorced from mystery we simply can't stand not knowing? Are we afraid and, if so, of what? If there is any fear of being known so deeply that your shadows become familiar, remember this: dark are the shadows that hide and keep the secrets of the universe and Earthy aliveness. Can you see the beauty that transpires in the dark?

Question:

What beauty have you experienced where there is little visible light?

Affirmation:

I am a wonder with shine and shadow.

Noticing:

What are you noticing today about the way you relate to darkness?

Offering

What we perceive as darkness is always related to light and luminosity. Visible light—what can be seen with human eyes—only makes up .0035%[3] of all known light waves. This means that most of what we see as dark is actually luminous in other ways. Inextricably, light is intertwined with darkness, not separate from it. Let us welcome it. Let us receive the goodness in every form of light and name its being. The heat your body gives off signals your aliveness and can be seen in infrared waves. *Let there be light*! When you get your picture taken with X-rays, you can see parts of your body typically encased in non-visible luminosity. *Let there be light*! In small amounts, ultraviolet waves aid our bodies in functioning wholly[4]. *Let there be light*! *Let there be darkness that yet contains light.*

WONDER

Question:

What is it like to consider dark and light as siblings or two parts of a whole instead of enemies?

Affirmation:

Even in darkness, I am light.

Noticing:

What are you noticing today about welcoming the dark?

8

Offering

Black holes are some of my favorite entities in the universe. Science still hasn't learned enough to tell the whole of their story. Something we do know, though, is their storied connection to quasars. Quasars are cores of galaxies that are extraordinarily luminous across the entire electromagnetic spectrum. That means they are super bright in visible light waves, radio waves, infrared waves, and every other way we understand light protons to exist. Here's the curious thing—these ultra luminous galactic cores are powered by light-eating black holes. I won't get into the science of that (but please go look it up, it's super interesting). I *will* get into the awe of it: the very entity that swallows every material thing, including every type of electromagnetic wave, is what powers the most vastly luminous object in the universe[5].

Question:

What "both/and" realities in your life are supportive and function well together?

Affirmation:

I am expansive and full of wonder.

Noticing:

What are you noticing today in creation that stokes awe in you?

Offering

Rest, growth, dreams, and secrets find a place to nestle and be nourished in darkness. Can our awe find its place there too? Moreso than fearful respect, can darkness draw out of us a wondrous admiration as light does? There is no rejuvenating rest, deepening of roots, or transformative dreaming without the presence of darkness. And while we don't understand all the mechanics of what happens in the dark, we know there isn't much that happens without it. Be jaw-droppingly, wow-inducingly inspired by the darkness. We may discover its necessity is rivaled only by its sister, the light.

Question:

When does darkness conjure fear in you instead of wonder?

Affirmation:

I am in awe of the mysteries I do not understand.

Noticing:

What are you noticing today about your relationship with fear in contrast to your relationship with wonder?

Offering

You might have heard the phrase "you have galaxies inside you." You, The Galaxy, have a breadth of *at least* thousands of lightyears. Within your galactic being are myriad stars, planets, asteroids, comets, gaseous clouds, and stellar nurseries. You are varied in cosmic ways, holding expanses of darkness and spaciousness as well as intense density and light. If we soar through the communities of celestial entities that comprise your galactic existence toward your center, there is a dense, deeply gravitational core of dignity holding all of it in place—your intrinsic worthiness. No core, no galaxy.

Question:

What expands for you when you consider yourself a galaxy?

Affirmation:

I am inherently vast and intrinsically worthy.

Noticing:

What are you noticing today about what feels true to you?

Offering

I venture that in The Eternal's vision, the whole electromagnetic —or light—spectrum is one of delight. Simply seeing you at any of the seven types of light on the spectrum gives great pleasure. Note, Beloved: Not everyone has this vision of seeing you in your total luminosity. Some deny your radiance even when you are shining right before them. Yet those with eyes to see the wavelengths on the delight spectrum see you with brilliance, glowing from places that read as non-luminous to the naked eye. May you have eyes that see your luminosity and name yourself Beloved and Delighted In. May you have eyes to see the divine luminosity of others and, as kin, call them Beloved also. May we remind one another that, when we forget our light, deny our light, or try to hide in the shadows, even the darkness shines as light.

Question:

What is your relationship to delight?

Affirmation:

I am full of delight.

Noticing:

What are you noticing about the presence of light where it's easier to focus on what's non-luminous in yourself and others?

"Life creates conditions conducive to life."

Janine Benyus
Biomimicry: Innovation Inspired by Nature

Offering

I say to The Stars: you are faithful. Millions and billions of Earth-years committed to being exactly who you are. You, The Stars, move in and out of your seasons of life without struggle but with acceptance. In death, you resolve in your powerful ending that all the bits of you will continue on a trajectory toward being known in different ways. Here on Earth, reconstituted with water and Imago Dei—the Divine image—you, The Stars, come alive in us. May we learn from your brilliance, from your uniqueness and dignity, from your acceptance of change and of death, and from your hope in resurrection. May we learn from you by being connected to our bodies and every body throughout creation. For you, The Stars, are alive in each of us as you are always alive in the sky, day or night.

Question:

How do the stars inspire connection in you?

Affirmation:

I am connected to my body, a physical resurrection of Stardust.

Noticing:

What are you noticing today about being your brilliant self?

Offering

Watching shows about space makes me feel small in the very best way. Not the smallness that's shame-y and trivializes. I mean the smallness that places me knowingly and specifically without making my existence swollen or overly significant. I am me in the utter vastness of creation. One singular human expression of The Eternal in this blink of time on this particular planet, I matter in many contexts. This "mattering" feels oriented toward Ubuntu—the Bantu word often translated "I am because we are."[6] What a beautiful way to matter—because of belonging, because of tethering. Because of the existence of other beings. While I may not have an effect on Andromeda—a neighboring galaxy set to collide with The Milky Way in about 4.5 billion years—I welcome an expansion of Ubuntu to include this cosmic entity in my mattering. We think so much of our connection primarily to other humans. What if our connection to the plants, the water, the stars, and the galaxies was just as strong and mattered just as much? What if "I am because *they* are"?

Question:

What more-than-human entity connects you to a sense of significance and belonging?

Affirmation:

I am, because the plants, the water, the stars, and the galaxies are.

Noticing:

What are you noticing today about your smallness?

Offering

"And now I feel like I know a very magical secret," Shonda Rhimes says in her 2016 TedTalk[7]. "Well, let's not get carried away. It's just love. That's all it is. No magic. No secret. It's just love. It's just something we forgot." Understandably, Rhimes quickly goes from "a magical secret" to "just love." Magical secrets require special knowledge and access. But in making it "just love," suddenly, the abundance of it is made known, and it—the love—becomes available to all. Not just to the Shonda Rhimeses of the world with all sorts of special access but to the yous and the mes as well. It's so beautiful—why do we have to be reminded? What makes us forget?

Question:
What makes you forget the abundance of "just love"?

Affirmation:
I am surrounded and filled by the abundance of Love.

Noticing:
What are you noticing that reminds you of the "just love" in your world?

Offering

I don't know if you know this, but... you are made of stars. Literally. In ultra-simplified layperson terms, here's what I mean: A star (or stars) died and released loads of energy. This energy carried the elements from within the star—like calcium, iron, and carbon—through the universe and eventually to Earth before Earth became inhabitable. Presumably, these very elements from stars are part of the reason *why* the Earth is inhabitable at all. So, quite literally, what's inside of you originates from a millions-year-old supernova[8].

Question:
How does being made of literal stardust affect your self-image?

Affirmation:
I am a reflection of the cosmic here on Earth.

Noticing:
What are you noticing today about the hardiness of creation?

Offering

There are waves in the fabric of space and time that originate at the universe's birth. This primordial movement of the universe is moving us and everything in existence like a low, guttural humming. The waves aren't perceptible without highly sensitive instruments[9], but knowing that you buzz in rhythm with the entirety of the universe... does something to you. Now it could do something to your ego, but it could also do something to your enoughness. With the utmost gentleness, the universe is wooing you into its rhythm. It's a rhythm marked by the slow creation of a 13-billion-year-old cosmos that brings forth phenomena like stellar nurseries and question-mark-shaped galaxies. And tiny phenomena like you and like me.

Question:

What does it mean for you to be in imperceptible rhythm with the entire cosmos?

Affirmation:

I am enough.

Noticing:

What are you noticing today about your *enoughness*?

Offering

A neutron star is what remains of a massive star after it dies in a supernova explosion. This remnant is the core of the once-massive star that collapsed down to about 20 kilometers. Neutron stars are wildly dense and spin at a dizzying astronomical rate. Textured similar to a smooth iron orb, it's got an ultra-strong, rapidly rotating magnetic field. The neutron star is powerful with its own life as a continuation of the story of a certain star[10]—and yet it exists as a direct result of *death*. Death is not the star of your story; the core of who you are is. Each of us experiences so many deaths along our journey. Whether we are burying a loved one, pieces of a dream, or a belief in a certain kind of safety, death becomes a passage to the subsequent version of ourselves—the one that has been changed by the prospect of a new chapter in our story.

Question:
What is your relationship to rebirth?

Affirmation:
I am alive in a cycle of life and death.

Noticing:
What are you noticing about the similarities between the neutron star's story and yours?

Offering

Marcie Alvis Walker wrote an Instagram post[11] in 2019 that I just love. She speaks of her wonder for the atheist and agnostic, noting that when fellow people-of-faith ask questions that tend toward slotting her and others into amorphous categories, she replies, "Who cares? We are made of stars!!!!" The Stars have wooed us into wonder, reminding us of what every single person, animal, and plant are built from—stardust and water. Our brains love a good category. Many specifics are fun to share, giving clues to the world around us about who we are without making our hearts too vulnerable in new situations. And... maybe sometimes it would be fun to answer a question that probes in unwanted ways with, "Who cares? You and me—we are made of stars!"

WONDER

Question:

What identities do you hold that remind you of your stardust origins?

Affirmation:

I am made of stardust.

Noticing:

What are you noticing today about what makes you feel safe enough to be known?

32

"It has been said that we are Star beings in human form. We have journeyed from the Cosmos and landed here, earth-bound in a body, and given unique instructions on how to spend our time on this planet."

Asha Frost
You Are The Medicine: 13 Moons of Indigenous Wisdom, Ancestral Connection, and Animal Spirit Guidance

Offering

The simplicity of looking at the night sky becomes complicated the closer we (or I?) get to the city and to busyness. The more my gaze stays at my eye level, the harder it is to justify looking up. A part of me can feel like it's frivolous to not keep my eyes on what's right in front of me. There is so much to see right in front of us. Recently, much of it has been tragic. I've been straining for the simple, the wonder, the divinity. Where is the brilliance we seek when everything illuminated is about the dark of death? Hopelessness drawing close, I hear The Stars calling: *Look up.*

Question:

When did you last look up at night and linger?

Affirmation:

I am called by The Stars.

Noticing:

What are you noticing about how wonder affects feelings of being overwhelmed?

Offering

Friend, I want you to be in awe of the cosmos. When you look up —or see pictures from a telescope, or hear a creation story, or just consider the vastness of existence—I hope it leaves you with your mouth wide open and no words to say. Secondarily, I want you to be deeply astounded by your connection to it all. The cosmos doesn't exist for humans; we are not the center of the universe. Yet, we are here with—and a part of—the cosmos. You are here, and that means something. How you got here—all the complicated processes required throughout space-time for you to be here *right now*—is an amazing, lovely, and awe-filled story.

Question:

Where do you usually start your origin story?

Affirmation:

I am connected to the vast cosmos.

Noticing:

What are you noticing today that expands your awareness beyond what is right in front of you?

Offering

After seeing the Moon and a nebula through a telescope set up in a university quad, I was shaking, and I wanted to cry, but no one else was crying, so I tried to hold it together. Then I stood in line at another telescope and looked at the Moon again. Then I stood in line at another telescope, unsure of what it was pointing at. While I waited, I looked up. I kept looking up. I couldn't stop looking up. And then a prayer bubbled up. I've prayed this prayer before. It felt honest and aged inside me, a bit worn like an old coat or a well-known story: *May I always be in awe.*

Question:

What is your petition or request in the moments you want to hold on to?

Affirmation:

I am willing to stay in wonder.

Noticing:

What are you noticing today when you look up?

WELCOME

Offering

A Love Note to The Stars: Humans may be how the universe knows itself[12], but truly we are only *a* way. Honestly, I can't know myself without the greater living whole—including you, The Stars. For millennia, we have looked to you to understand who we are. To plot not just location but also context. To navigate not just the seas but also ourselves. To become familiar with the seasons of the years, our communities, and our personhood. We have always known you because you have always known us. Because of you, The Stars, we are.

Question:

What do the stars help you understand about humanity?

Affirmation:

I am a descendant of stars.

Noticing:

What are you noticing today about the night sky?

Offering

Our sweet blue dot exists in a system with our natural satellite, the Moon. This paired system is in a dance with multiple planets all in an orbital tango with our Sun. Our Solar System is on the Orion Arm of the Milky Way Galaxy[13]. And our galaxy is one of an estimated 2 trillion galaxies—dots of their own in our immeasurable universe[14]. The overwhelming wonder of this has become a comfort, a welcomed stretching of my imagination and blowing of my mind. We live and move and have our being here, at this intersection of space and time. We look through our telescopes into a universe contextualized from our perspective: the blue-dot perspective. It's only one out of countless, but it's ours, and we are here.

Question:

When has your imagination been stretched and reshaped by wonder?

Affirmation:

I am here.

Noticing:

What are you noticing today about your place in the universe?

Offering

The Spindle Galaxy[15] is 44 million light years away from Earth. This means it has taken its light that long to get to us. 44 million years is the age of the light we see in images of that galaxy today. Since we are not the sole center of the universe, we know the Spindle Galaxy has purpose completely untethered to us. As the Spindle Galaxy is contentedly being its lovely luminous self, what can 44-million-year-old light mean to us? What's the point of us not only seeing the light but also knowing some parts of the light's story, as well as knowing that its source no longer exists as we see it (because we are seeing it as it was 44 million years ago)? If the ancestral light of a galaxy can exist—without diffusing, with a clarity of its source as brilliant and wonder-full as it was when the light first left—for millions of years, what can we imagine of our own ancestral light?

Question:

What are the most important aspects of the legacy you want to be known for 44 generations from now?

Affirmation:

I am luminous and wonder-full.

Noticing:

What are you noticing today about the legacy you are observing of those who have passed on?

Offering

Consider the 100 million black holes in the Milky Way[16] and their horizons. Do you know what they share with our planet? An origin story. I LOVE collective origin stories. Creation stories. Cultural cosmologies. Scientific storying called "theory" is built on what we *know* as we make strong hypotheses about what we *don't*. As humans, we have always looked up with wonder and awe. It's as though something within was pulling us—no, tethering us—to the first line of an unknown story. And not just to the stories of our existence, but to the existence of *everything*. From this tethering, we have created myriad sacred narratives about cosmic connections that express themselves in our specific locale of the universe. We've looked to the horizon 100 million times and knew what touched it also touched us.

Question:

What reminds you of your tether to the whole of creation?

Affirmation:

I am a descendant of generations of wonderers.

Noticing:

What are you noticing today about our origin stories?

"...the cosmos is within us. We are made of star-stuff. We are a way for the universe to know itself."

Carl Sagan
Cosmos

Offering

A petition to The Stars: Help us to love the darkness, for this is your home. Darkness is where you are born, where you live, and where you die. Darkness is your cultural context, the mother of your generations. As she is to you, may she be to us as well.

Question:

What do you love about darkness?

Affirmation:

I am formed in the dark.

Noticing:

What are you noticing about your relationship to the dark?

Offering

"You're looking for a cluster of four stars," the telescope operator instructed. "And there is a cloud around the cluster. That's a nebula where stars are being born." *Bruh, you don't have to tell me. Don't you read my writing?* No, I did not say that. Instead I took a deep breath, leaned in, and saw stars like I never had. They had a sharpness and texture you don't see with the naked eye. They seemed alive. It seemed like they had breath—a breath you can't capture with even the best camera. No, you have to see them breathe for yourself. And then I saw *the faint cloud*: a nebula, the womb of stars. My breath caught, and I tried desperately not to cry.

Question:

Can you be still long enough to notice the breath of what's around you, like the bugs, the wind, the plants?

Affirmation:

I am alive along with the entirety of the cosmos.

Noticing:

What are you noticing today about the aliveness of more-than-human beings?

Offering

If wonder and awe are twins, then curiosity is their sibling. When the interest that leads to inquiry grows up with wonder and awe, it's hard to get too far from a genuine childlikeness. As new beings on the Earth, children have a two-part job: 1) Follow what's interesting. 2) Bask in its wonder. Many of us as adults become trained to find the right answer to our curiosity rather than being wowed by it. We value being right so much that we trade it in for our natural inclination toward amazement. Trade it back! Let imagination and openheartedness give birth to curiosity, wonder, and awe. Like a child, they can show you the way.

Question:

What for you serves as a direct line to childlike wonder?

Affirmation:

I am naturally inclined toward awe.

Noticing:

What are you noticing today about openheartedness?

Offering

Dandelions—especially when they turn into those feathery fluff-balls—make me think about supernovas and our connection to them. Well, at least one of them. Eons ago, a particular massive star tried to fuse iron in its core. The Celestial Gardener[17], with whimsy and joy, saw this cosmic dandelion was ready. Eyes closed, with a pause, I wonder what the Gardener wished for. What hope would the star seeds carry lightyears away in space and time? A deep inhale, then The Celestial Gardener blew breath out. The star went supernova, flinging the star seeds through space, carrying the hope and joy of The Gardener to Earth.

Question:

What are you wishing for these days?

Affirmation:

I am the result of star seeds landing on Earth.

Noticing:

What are you noticing today about whimsy and joy?

Offering

The story of Jesus of Nazareth tells of an embodied shattering of the idea of "Life & Death," calling it an incomplete sentence. It's an unfinished understanding. Cosmically, it's Life & Death & *Life*. This seems to be a normal reality. Resurrection is so common among the stars that there are multiple ways the physical star has an afterlife[18]. For massive stars, the body it sheds from its first life carries the seeds for the new beginnings of stars, planets, gardens, and—quite phenomenally—you and me. Resurrection is so common that the moon has cyclical phases where light leaves and returns over and over and over again. Resurrection is so common that there is a supernova remnant—from the death of a star—named the Butterfly Nebula[19], after an Earthly symbol of rebirth. The cosmos affirms this universal promise of Life & Death & *Life*.

Question:

What have you been invited to consider about life after death?

Affirmation:

I am a product of the death of a star.

Noticing:

What are you noticing today about what is common?

Offering

Some of us are very familiar with red clay. It's the kind of "dirt" that stains whatever it touches. When that red clay makes a permanent home on your clothes, the iron of that place will forever be with you. Interestingly enough, when a star dies in a supernova explosion, we know there are multiple possible results, one of which is a neutron star. Do you know what is at the core of a neutron star? A super dense ball of liquid matter with a crust of smooth... iron[20]. The same element in our clay, our humus, and our bodies is also present in the cosmos in the life and death of stars. When you name yourself an Earthly One, you also name yourself a Cosmic One. Being of the Earth confirms that you are also of The Stars.

Question:

What are the most resonant ways you are named?

Affirmation:

I am of the Earth, so I am of The Stars.

Noticing:

What are you noticing today that grounds you in wonder?

Offering

Carl Sagan talks about Earth being where "the matter of the cosmos"[21] has become "alive and aware,"[22] which is utterly staggering to my Earthling soul. Wondrously, we are made of the stuff of stars. YOU are made of stars—and that's not hyperbole. Drawing from the imagination of some ancient theologians and synthesizing their narrative with science[23], here's how I'd tell it: The Creator of the universe caused stardust to fall to this blue dot we call Earth. That stardust would then mix with heat and water to produce life, which the aforementioned Creator would breathe into and teach the human Earthling how to tend the very Earth from which they were formed. That, friends, is what I'd call a science of lovingkindness.

Question:

What happens when you simply sit with the idea that what you are made of originates from an actual star?

Affirmation:

I am the matter of the cosmos, alive and aware.

Noticing:

What are you noticing today about story and science?

Second Cycle

"As humans and animals, we easily turn
to nature to find something that was
either lost or wants to be found."

Rue Mapp
Nature Swagger

"To pronounce a blessing on something, it is important to see it as it is...[a stick] is no less than the artery of a tree that you are holding in your hand."

Barbara Brown Taylor
An Altar in the World: A Geography of Faith

Offering

We're at the beach, seeing bodies bathed by our star, the Sun, and caressed by our ocean. The shells and sand underfoot are, for some beach walkers, the only Earth they'll let their bare feet touch. When we take our shoes off, do we make the beach holy? Do we make the wet sand a sacred place? Maybe where the ocean touches the shore is a thin place, where bodies of land and bodies of water meet. It's the place where holy bodies are welcomed by water and light. We see a beautiful, fat Black woman in a bathing suit, enjoying her place in her body. Though I am not a fat woman, I use the term "fat" in solidarity with those who are reclaiming the word to highlight the inherent wonder located in their particular body. Her body is as beachy as the slender person in a bikini. Both beach bodies. Tiny fish dart around in the shallow waters we wade in. Also, beach bodies. Young and old, with skin tones, abilities, and neuro-capacities across the spectrum. All beautiful. All beach bodies.

Question:

What is your relationship like with your body when in public?

Affirmation:

I am here to occupy all the space in my wondrous body.

Noticing:

What are you noticing about your response to others publicly enjoying being in their body?

Offering

There are so many kinds of bodies. Celestial bodies like planets, stars, and asteroids. Terrestrial bodies like microbes, plants, and humans. Bodies of water and bodies of land. Within bodies there are entire systems with millions of tiny bodies. Bodies across creation are different sizes, shine in different wavelengths, and have a variety of textures. The complexity and diversity of all the bodies in the cosmos only exist because of one particular element. Hydrogen is the base of every body. No hydrogen, no body. Wherever and whenever you think the beginning is, hydrogen was there (or fractions of a second after[24]), and hydrogen has been a part of the creative, evolutionary process ever since.

Question:

What is an essential element of your origin story?

Affirmation:

I am wholly essential in my whole body.

Noticing:

What are you noticing today that *includes* instead of *others*?

Offering

I'd been practicing some pretty deep, soul-shifting courage *for months* and my body was tired. As is her custom, my body asked me for rest. *Can we just breathe for a while? Let all this work we've done settle down into the toes? I am holding all of it up here, and I want it to take time to settle.* "Up here" was in my chest and my belly. And when you are holding stuff in your chest and belly, guess what there's less room for? Breath. When I slowed enough to reconnect to my breath, what I was feeling and needing came up, expecting my attention. I'm grateful I've learned to listen—most of the time. While the internal shifting settles, I don't want to just remember to breathe; I want to take slow, deep, wondrous breaths. I want to drink in each breath like cool water, because it is water and connection to my own body, to every other human, to the trees, and to the greater living whole.

Question:

Are you willing to pause right now and take three deep, slow breaths?

Affirmation:

I am connected to my body and my breath.

Noticing:

What are you noticing today about what is calling for your attention?

Offering

In Rev. Dr. Randy Woodley's book, *Becoming Rooted* [25], one meditation invites the reader to spend at least one hour in silence outdoors in the natural world. So I did. I welcomed the time alone, surrounded by creation with my senses focused in the silence. These moments are never just about what you *aren't* doing, but more so about what you *are* doing. What did I do in self-imposed silence? I listened. I noticed. I breathed. I smiled. I wondered. It wasn't perfect. I got distracted with that ongoing internal conversation... about what to cook for dinner and what I should do with my hair in the coming week. Each time, thankfully, I was able to reground and come back to the present. I was slow. I stopped often. I looked up. It was a practice worthy of becoming a regular part of me connecting to myself and the more-than-human whole—engaging the restfulness I need to show up well in my day-to-day living.

Question:

Are there disciplines that help you notice wonder?

Affirmation:

I am open to the presence of wonder.

Noticing:

What are you noticing today that is slow?

Offering

Keep your openhearted curiosity going, my friend. You can ask why and you can say "wow." You can ask why over and over—like a 3-year-old—because you let wonder run ahead, gripping your curiosity tightly in hand. Ask why until all there is left is "wow." You—with all your adulting and responsibilities and serious decisions to make—are worthy of daily wows. May your curiosity lead to wonder, never frustration, and only rarely lead to certainty (strictly when necessitated). You don't have to cling to certainty. Some of us are choking certainty to death while hoping that, by force, we can get whatever we believe it gives. You can breathe instead, laugh even, if you want. Let your why wander you to a wow.

Question:

What is the last thing that made you audibly say "wow"?

Affirmation:

I am worthy of daily wows.

Noticing:

What are you noticing today about your openness to childlikeness?

Offering

There were multiple telescopes around the small quad, with the first one I encountered pointed at the moon. It was a clear night, and at slightly more than half full, she was bright and beautiful to the naked eye. When I first glanced through the telescope, I immediately recoiled because of the awe. Seeing the Moon's detail and brightness with my eyes so vividly that I felt I could reach out and touch her... it was too much. I took a deep breath and leaned into the telescope's finder again. It took every cell in my body not to weep. I was breathless, speechless, disoriented. I was enveloped in awe.

Question:

When was the last time wonder caused a visceral reaction in you, like an involuntary recoiling, disorientation, or even a burst of tearful joy?

Affirmation:

I am open to wonder taking my breath away.

Noticing:

What are you noticing today about what makes you stop in your tracks?

Offering

I'm not sure if Dacher Keltner, professor and author of the book, *Awe*, would agree with me, but I use the word *wonder* interchangeably with the word *awe*. Keltner shares extensively about how science can measure awe and that makes my nerdy heart super happy. I can geek out about all the research tracking where we find awe and how we experience wonder. And... science isn't needed to identify wonder. Your body feels it when you're in the presence of natural grandeur. Our nervous systems sync up when we move or experience wonder as a collective[26]. Science is a kind of storyteller, naming characters in our shared story we are already quite familiar with: wonder, awe, and that audible "wow."

Question:

What bodily sensations help you mark moments of awe?

Affirmation:

I am a storyteller of wonder.

Noticing:

What are you noticing today about the somatic presence of wonder?

"When I fear the universe, I fear myself. When I love and am in awe of the universe, I love and am in awe of myself."

adrienne maree brown
Emergent Strategy: Shaping Change, Changing Worlds

Offering

The edelweiss flower is scarce among the extensive presence of her siblings: dandelion, daisy, and sunflower. Each flower is heaven on Earth, the cosmic reflected in the terrestrial. As a member of the "Star Flower" family, edelweiss doesn't just bloom when it's cold. It flourishes in snowy, rocky, and rugged terrain like the French Alps, which are cold. Like, *Imma go pick that flower and try not to die* cold. There is wisdom and gift given to us from edelweiss, the Star Flower that blooms on the snowy, rocky mountainside[27]. Edelweiss is a reminder that life does exist in the winter, even if it's scarce. The rareness elicits songs about its very existence[28], baffling us into musings of life and beauty springing forth from the bitter cold.

Question:
What is alive for you in this season?

Affirmation:
I am abundant even in bitter seasons.

Noticing:
What are you noticing today that is surprising you?

Offering

Transformation can bring you into places and ways of being you hadn't imagined before the journey. A few years ago, during a walk on the beach, the seashells inspired this musing: *What I do matters to the sea. Who I am matters to the creatures big and small that I will never meet in person. Seashells are beautiful reminders of the little beings who once inhabited them. These tiny creations give more gifts than can be realized—including their discarded shells on the beach...My breath matters. I am made of stars. Water is my original elder. And there are dignified creatures in the waters and lands I may never get to, but the effects of my living will.* The same is true for you, my friend. Wherever you are on the journey—maybe even sitting on the side of the path for an extended break—may you breathe deep, gaze at the sky, give thanks to the water. May you learn from the more-than-human, care about their well-being, and connect in a reciprocity. And in all this, Love. Receive Love, give Love, rest in Love, and live through Love.

Question:

What is a recent aha moment you've had on your journey?

Affirmation:

I am living in and through Love.

Noticing:

What are you noticing today that is small but has an effect on you?

Offering

One of the things I think is so enchanting about Jesus of Nazareth is where he places death in the story. In Jesus's enfleshed resurrection, he proclaims that death doesn't get to tell the end of our story. Not the end of mine and not the end of yours. Not in this life or whatever comes after our last breath. Every neutron star—the lively rebirth, if you will, of a massive star that died—agrees: death will not tell the end of the story. There is no escaping death being *part* of the story. But the point of resurrection is that, though death may be present, it will not be the star. Jesus will be the star. An edelweiss flower blooming in the dead of winter will be the star. You and I—we will be the neutron star of our story.

Question:

What has felt like death in your life that you have lived beyond?

Affirmation:

I am the star of my story.

Noticing:

What are you noticing today about the role hope plays in your story?

Offering

The fluffy joy-ball that is commonly known as a dandelion, my kids and I call a wish. When we see one ready to be plucked and blown like a birthday candle, we say, "Look! A wish!" Just like the wish is an ingenious way dandelions continue their species, a supernova—the explosive death of a massive star—sends out the seeds of the cosmic garden. This explosion hurdles the seeds for future stars, planets, solar systems, and galaxies through the cosmic landscape. Dandelions don't explode, so they've been in a generations-long entanglement with humanity, ensuring their storied presence for ages to come.

Question:

When was the last time you partnered with the procreation of dandelions and made a wish?

Affirmation:

I am an active participant in the ongoing support of life on the Earth.

Noticing:

What are you noticing today about how you affect the more-than-human world around you?

Offering

Imagine a wilderness. Consider the root word here: wild. Imagine a natural wild. Imagine how the sunlight dances and where raindrops touch the Earth in this wild place. Who is there? And, by who, I mean every more-than-human being. Breathe in the smell of this wild place. You are here. Enter in fully. You don't have to be afraid or attempt to domesticate the wildness surrounding you. Instead, let wonder lead your curiosity. What if the wilderness isn't for you to form or to calm, but it's where *you* are formed? Instead of dominating the wilderness into your own image, what if the wilderness is offering to change and develop you? What do you say to this offer? Be in this wilderness as a place, not as a goal or project. Consider that *you* are the project, and this more-than-human wild is a guide in the deepening of your wonder.

Question:

Of the questions posed in this reflection, which is calling most to you?

Affirmation:

I am present and willing to let the wilderness deepen me.

Noticing:

What are you noticing today about what is alive around you, independent of your efforts?

Offering

Primordial darkness seems to be tethered to womb-iness where existence gestates, is nurtured, and sustained. We know this tethering in an Earthy way as well. Put a seed in the darkness of the ground, and it springs forth into a new cycle of life. In the darkness of our bodies, microscopic interminglings start the formation of a new human. Within the seamless container of the egg, various beings find their beginning. The primordial darkness of a cosmic scale is recreated in and around us in the microscopic. Womby darkness is near and a deep part of our existence.

Question:

Where are you finding the wonder of the womb?

Affirmation:

I am well-nurtured in the dark.

Noticing:

What are you noticing today about life being connected to the dark?

Offering

Throughout my professional life and written works I talk a lot—a *lot*—about dignity, which I define as the intrinsic worth and value each being carries that cannot be taken away. I lean into this foundational element of our being because I have experienced too many of us—including myself—walking around this blue dot, this humusy Earth, desperately unsure of a deeply necessary certainty: our worthiness. With this need to focus on worthiness, I utilize the vehicle of teaching from a foundation of dignity to center each being's worth as primary, unshakable, and unquestionable. You may *do* questionable things, but you *being* worthy is no question. Address what you do; affirm who you are.

Question:

What has made you question your worthiness?

Affirmation:

I am valuable and worthy simply because I exist.

Noticing:

What are you noticing today about addressing what you do and affirming who you are?

"Cosmology requires multigenerational patience."

Dr. Chanda Prescod-Weinstein
*The Disordered Cosmos: A Journey into
Dark Matter, Spacetime, and Dreams
Deferred*

Offering

What happens when the horizon becomes the first line of our origin stories? In storytelling, we stitch the Earth to the Sky, making sense of our existence and place in the vastness of the universe. From cosmic eggs to spoken words, cosmologies through place and time insist that our existence is wrapped up in the existence of what is toward and beyond the horizon[29]. The sea kisses the sunset; the stars touch the ground; and the stories we tell dance with the life of the cosmos.

Question:

When you consider what's beyond that line where the sky meets the Earth, what bubbles up inside of you?

Affirmation:

I am of a cosmic and terrestrial origin story.

Noticing:

What are you noticing comes to mind when you look out or look up?

Offering

Ground is the tangible expression of place. Many believe there are specific areas of ground that are so holy that the only proper contact with them is to have nothing between our feet and that sacred, specific Earth. In this, holiness beckons us closer to the ground, not away from it. What made the ground holy is often a significant event in space-time that changed us forever. Nothing is degrading about being close to the ground. The sacred calls us not just closer to the place but to allow our stories to be rooted and grounded in it. It is honorable to move through the world with groundedness and rooting into place. Humility isn't about lowliness. It's about knowing who, whose, and *where* you are.

Question:

Where is the Earth holy for you?

Affirmation:

I am humble, confidently knowing who, whose, and where I am.

Noticing:

What are you noticing today about humility?

Offering

Growing up, I had a beautiful relationship with my hyperlocal place: the backyard of my childhood home. You'd have been worried I'd grow roots and leaves as much as I was out there. Feet in the grass, hands on tree trunks, eyes to the cotton-puffed sky. This was my place, and I flourished. An only child, I played and pretended, sang and ran, imagined and made wishes. Outside. My favorite place on Earth. Actually, I may have grown roots and leaves, nourished in that patch of land.

Question:

What place has nourished you?

Affirmation:

I am root and leaf nourished by the land.

Noticing:

What are you noticing today about outside?

Offering

There is a large family of flowers called the Asteraceae. Aster is Greek for star, so their family name is Star Flower (!). Among the many kin in the Star Flower family are daisies, dandelions, sunflowers, and the edelweiss. This is of interest to me. Our daisies, dandelions, and sunflowers signal sun and warmth, the colorful summer blooming. But the edelweiss is notably different. The French and Italians name this flower *the star of the Alps*[30], which blooms on snowy mountainsides in the dead of winter.

Question:

In which season do you find yourself flourishing?

Affirmation:

I am a seasonal creature.

Noticing:

What are you noticing today that is in bloom?

Offering

What of us being named the Earthly ones? What inextricable connection is made when we are named directly after our place— our place in the cosmos, our place on this blue dot, our place in the more-than-human world and its cycles? The Earthly Ones. Even in sci-fi B-movies, we are called after our place: Earthlings. Let it not just be because this planet is where the green aliens would find us. Let it be because the Earth is our home and our connection, our name, and our origin on a cellular level.

Question:

What does it mean to you to be "of the Earth"?

Affirmation:

I am of the Earth, and it is good.

Noticing:

What are you noticing today that makes you feel a part of your place?

Offering

Dear Earth, please forgive us. There is this stage—like a teenager/early-twenty-something stage—when we think we know better than Mama. But when Mama moves from wisdom and authenticity, you realize Mama knew more than you gave Mama credit for, loving from a place of care, wise consideration, and ebb and flow. Earth, you have known so, so much more than I—we—have given you credit for. Who has already learned this lesson? What older, more-than-human siblings honor that which you have *always* known?

Question:

When have you been influenced by the care and wisdom of the Earth?

Affirmation:

I am honoring of Earth's wisdom.

Noticing:

What are you noticing today from more-than-human beings?

Offering

How can you live connected to awe? Pay her your attention. Set rhythmic reminders, like our ancestors did and so many still do. From giving thanks to all the beings that made it possible to eat the food on your plate to gathering at a solstice or equinox event, you can create rhythms that match the cadence of the Earth and the Stars to honor the gifts we receive because of them. It is easy to live disconnected from awe... until it's not. Once you realize that awe is not only somewhere outside of you but that you are directly tethered to it, that changes things. My hope is it changes *you*. I hope you start to see awe everywhere. In the purple flower, that bright star, your laughter, and their smile. May you see and feel the connection of the worlds right before you and the worlds millions of light years away.

Question:
How are you already aware of how you are tethered to awe?

Affirmation:
I am filled with awe.

Noticing:
What are you noticing today that is common and awesome?

"Each tree, like every other creature, exists in relationship to its surroundings. We are all intricately linked to all of creation. We are related to the world around us."

Rev. Dr. Randy Woodley
Becoming Rooted: One Hundred Days of Reconnecting with Sacred Earth

Offering

In the story of Jesus of Nazareth's burial in a garden and resurrection in the same place, there is a day between the two events: a Saturday. Saturday wasn't the day for death *or* for life. Saturday was the day to sit, to stay, to sabbath at the table of grief. Saturdays in the garden are rough. Saturdays in the garden are when we go out ready to tend to life, but find that there is death that needs our attention. Spending Saturdays in the garden is when we feel mocked by the blooming flowers and buzzing pollinators, because our life is marked with lifelessness, death, and a gaze blurry with tears. Saturday is agony, desperation, hopelessness, and fear. Saturday is brokenheartedness—the kind that shatters you into a million pieces. I know why we—why *I*—don't want to commune at the table of grief, don't want to sabbath with dead hope. It's painful and devastating. No one wants the stillness of a Saturday to consider the promise of death.

Question:

Do you think wonder and grief cohabitate? If so, where? How?

Affirmation:

I am whole even when my heart is broken.

Noticing:

What are you noticing today about death?

Offering

Ajiri Aki wrote in her book *Joie*[31], "I always say there is power in gathering around a table because it is where our souls collide." Sometimes our most wonder-full connections are right across the table from us. You may be someone who wants to work their way around the table and have a conversation with every person there. You may be great at remembering names, which dish everyone liked the most, and what book or music is inspiring their moments. You may be someone who wants to go deep with one or two people the whole night. You want to find your spot at the table and just follow a one-on-one conversation until you've made a friend, feeling seen and known. You may have all the best jokes, the latest celebrity news, or the coolest hacks for "adulting." Whoever you are, show up at the table as your wondrous, phenomenal self. *You* are the magic at the table. You are the wonder and the joy.

Question:
When was the last time you met new people?

Affirmation:
I am magic as my wondrous self.

Noticing:
What are you noticing today about the power of a table?

Offering

Do you know what can punctuate a grand experience of wonder? The collective. The community. There are so many people, so many *different* people, of *different* ages, speaking *different* languages, at varying intersections you can't name or know simply from standing next to them. At a public astronomy night where anyone could come to look through a telescope, we were there in all our differences for one reason: The Night Sky. This brings forth a deep awe, too. When we come together in all our variety with the singular goal to marvel at the cosmos, there is a Oneness of wonder. *May we always always always be in awe.*

Question:
When have you experienced communal wonder?

Affirmation:
I am a part of the wonder-full whole.

Noticing:
What are you noticing today about our collective being-ness?

Offering

It is a miracle and gift, wondrous and unfathomable that we're all here. In *this* Milky Way galaxy, on *this* arm of the galaxy, in *this* single-star system, on *this* planet with *this* moon. We flourish here. What a grace and a gift to flourish at all. To be so aware of life being miraculous, we must write, paint, sing, and story-tell about all of existence. On a grand scale, the complexity of our interconnected, water-based life flourishes best here on this blue dot in this Milky Way. What a gift you are. You and I are we, and we are all here.

Question:

When you allow the wonder of life to have your attention, what are you drawn to create?

Affirmation:

I am here, and I am creative.

Noticing:

What are you noticing today about the miracles around you?

Offering

Dr. Gigi Khanyezi[32] has taught me and many others of the power one regulated nervous system has in a room full of nervous systems. All the science Dr. Khanyezi knows about this plus my experience point to a singularity of truth: We heal in community. More specifically, we *regulate* in community. In a theatre class, when my teacher asked me a question, I knew I was being invited to tell the truth, to wager that my classmates could and would be present with me as I confessed a pain I'd had the whole time we'd been together. I distinctly remember my choice: I could hide or I could be vulnerable. In that moment, I could choose to wear a mask or I could choose to bare my soul, but it was my split-second choice. Teary-eyed, I confessed one of the deepest fears that had gotten into an entanglement with my theatre love: belonging. Rather, *not* belonging. A communal energetic exhale let me know I wasn't alone, and I felt a regulation of my soul.

Question:

How has your community held you in your pain?

Affirmation:

I am safe with the people who help regulate my soul.

Noticing:

What are you noticing today about vulnerability and community?

Offering

We've been "archiving awe"—a phrase I'm borrowing from Dacher Keltner in his book, *Awe*—for thousands of years. In *Awe*, Keltner notes that around 100,000 years ago the human species started this cataloging with "language, symbols, music, and visual art." What is particularly interesting about this to me is what *preceded* the archiving of awe. As a newer species, we'd been navigating danger and the unknown together. The archival of awe emerges from the awe of our survival. Artists today keep this age-old commentary and cataloging going, reminding us of where we have come from and helping us imagine a future where we continue —together.

Question:

How do you personally archive awe?

Affirmation:

I am a future my ancestors imagined.

Noticing:

What are you noticing today about shared vision?

Offering

Rowan White, a Mohawk woman living on her ancestral lands, spoke with writer, embodiment teacher, and conflict facilitator Prentis Hemphill on Hemphill's podcast *Finding Our Way*[33]. White spoke vulnerably about her relationship to her place, sharing her experience of diaspora while in her ancestral place due to displacement from her people's cultural knowledge and experience. When displacement occurs, what of flourishing? Does flourishing become complicated? I would venture it does in different ways for each of us. What I know is that flourishing is a communal endeavor. Like roots and leaves, flourishing for us takes time, sunlight, water, and... Earth. Dear One, there is no flourishing without Earth—her wisdom, care, medicine, and rhythms.

Question:

What does flourishing taste, smell, sound, feel, and look like to you?

Affirmation:

I am continually supported by the generous Earth.

Noticing:

What are you noticing today about the communal nature of flourishing?

Third Cycle

"By your stories you are known."

Ken Liu
The Armies of Those I Love

"..if you are willing to take one meaningful step on your own behalf toward making a dream come true today, the Universe will meet you where you are and help you take two. The Universe will never shortchange you."

Leslie Odom, Jr.
Failing Up: How to Take Risks, Aim Higher, and Never Stop Learning

Offering

I'm naturally very serious-minded. I've found that the serious, pensive part of me has to get out in the yard to play hide and seek with wonder. The hum of the universe is Loving playfulness, is joy—and that joy is true even when you have to do the work, and clean the things, and go get groceries. More than true, this joy is accessible. It doesn't start with our "yes" to it; it's always there. Instead, our "yes" awakens us to the joy at the very fabric of the entire cosmos, and suddenly we are enveloped in the singing of the universe. It's in the rhythm of childlike joy where we live in tune with the tiny, imperceptible ways we rock and sway in the beat of space-time. May a deeply persistent "yes" be your answer to the question the universe has already asked you: Wanna play?

Question:

How is play trying to court you?

Affirmation:

I am worthy of putting play on my to-do list.

Noticing:

What are you noticing today about your natural relationship to joy?

Offering

Slow. Slow is a hard thing for me to hold on to. But you, Earth, don't do anything with speed. No, Earth, you move slowly, grow slowly, and your seasons take time. May I learn slowness and rhythm from you. I am *of* you, but now I want to be more *like* you. There is a difference, right? Can I be *of* you but not *like* you? Some stuff must just be in me like there are some things of me in my kids. They can't deny it or undo it; it's simply there. What of you, Earth, is in me? What of you is undeniable and irreversible in me? And how can I embrace it while living in a society that seems uninterested in being Earth-like, Earth-ly, Earth-y... you know, they not tryna be like they mama?

Question:

What aspects of you are similar to aspects of Earth?

Affirmation:

I am like Mother Earth, my mama.

Noticing:

What are you noticing today about how humans—individually or collectively—deny their inherent Earthiness?

Offering

I wonder what would happen if we returned to rhythms, to rituals, like the ones the Earth keeps. If we returned and relaxed into rhythms of seasons, rituals of slowness, lives that breathed deep. Not "in defiance of" only, or even primarily. But mainly because we are of the Earth. And slowness, rhythms, rituals, and rest are Earthy and terrestrial. In addition to being of and like her, belonging is the blanket Earth offers us. And really, I just want to stay curled up in that blanket of belonging, perched on Mother Earth's lap and wrapped in her arms, listening to her voice singing over me and over me and over us over and over and over. Earth, I love you. You are big and beautiful and exceeding abundantly more than enough. Thank you.

Question:

Have you ever let the Earth simply hold you?

Affirmation:

I am Earthy and can sync with the rhythms of my place.

Noticing:

What are you noticing today that has become a barrier to you living more Earth-centered?

Offering

There is a blue and black butterfly that visits me every year. Obviously, it's not the same butterfly, but whatever lineage of blue and black butterflies keep finding me year after year have become friends, guides even. I'm no taxonomist, but I'm pretty sure they are Harbor Goddesses (more commonly known as Red-spotted Purple Admiral[34], but I like Harbor Goddess better). I've embraced my storied relationship with this species of butterfly, one that reminds me there is more than what is right in front of me. And that more will always find me. Friend, there is more than the responsibilities screaming your name. If you're able to move into some quiet, you'll hear wonder is calling too—and the voice of wonder is all around. In the giggle of children, that sweet note from a colleague, in the sunlight peeking through the trees, and in the visitation from one we call Harbor Goddess, reminding you there is a shore beckoning you to notice and to rest.

Question:

Are there creatures who have a recurring and welcomed presence in your life?

Affirmation:

I am more than what I can get done.

Noticing:

What are you noticing today about what is calling to you?

Offering

For decades the universe was trying to woo me back to a place of singular and original Love—with play. Hell, the Eternal powers-that-be sent me a husband who was getting his PhD in play. As a budding cosplayer, an avid comic book reader, and a moonlighting salsa dancer, my now-husband-then-fiancé thought I had two heads when I said to him, "I don't do arbitrary fun." Add on top that my play needed to always have a *serious* purpose or outcome, and the universe thought I had two heads as well. I was only thinking with the cognitive one, but the rhythmic one beckoned me to dance. The almost imperceptible vibration of all things—a vibration whose origins align with the universe's beginnings—whispered to me in a million ways, "Don't forget the joy. Remember it's right here."

Question:

What outcome do you require of playfulness?

Affirmation:

I am ready to dance with the universe.

Noticing:

What are you noticing today about joy?

Offering

Wonder can be slow, like many other things. At times wonder may be triggered quickly, but it can linger for days, months, or even years. Have you ever recalled an awe-filled experience and felt your body and emotions re-experience their initial expression of wonder? Have you ever felt wonder grow over time during a long walk, conversation, or communal gathering? This is slow wonder. These are the awe-filled moments that aren't forced or manufactured— they simply happen. It's the body with all its interdependent systems connecting to the age-old shared experience of wonder. There is no rush to be awed, no race to find wonder. I don't think you have to *find* wonder at all. Friend, wonder is right here, where you are, and is illuminated when you become aware and welcome it.

Question:
How slow have you been lately?

Affirmation:
I am aware and welcoming of wonder.

Noticing:
What are you noticing today about memories of wonder?

Offering

There is a song from 2004 by retired singer/songwriter Bebo Norman[35] that I deeply connect to because of its utter insistence on community, specifically around waning hope. I get the disappointing reality-of-now that causes you to put your dreams at the end of your driveway for some stranger to take off your hands and out of your sight. What I've learned is a truth in the lyrics of this song: Like many other things, hope is a communal endeavor. The kind of community that offers hope for you to borrow is expansive, including beloveds that will hold you now, beings of past and present, entities of the Earth and the cosmos. The kind of community that helps you separate out wishful thinking from hopes that are the building blocks of our futures. Give your wishes to the meteorites that dissolve in Earth's atmosphere. Tell millions-of-years-old stars your dreams.

Question:

What hopes have you wanted to give up lately?

Affirmation:

I am a dreamer, and my dreams are nurtured in community.

Noticing:

What are you noticing today about how your community tends to hope?

"Healing brought me into a face-to-face confrontation with belonging, with the strategies I had developed to hide, the stories I told about not needing anyone that made the hiding easier. Healing had me admit that it was closeness I wanted, love and relationship and family who didn't ask me to hide."

Prentis Hemphill
"The Wisdom of Process" from
You Are Your Best Thing

Offering

I learned from Aomawa Shields, PhD about a shared reality people have with planets and ships: anchors. Shields speaks beautifully about this in the "Tides" chapter of her memoir, *Life On Other Planets*[36]. The element that accompanies each anchor is force. Not a coercive or oppressive force. A welcomed force that tethers Earth to the life-giving Sun and our tide-making Moon. The force that keeps a ship secure during a storm. And the anchor of people? I think we have many anchors. Some we find rust through pretty easily; some can't sustain the force we need to hold us steady. But wonder... wonder can be the life-giving, ebb-and-flow force that moves with us through our days. It can be our companion in the middle of the fiercest storms. On a night when the sky seems lifeless, it's that one stubborn electromagnetic pinprick piercing Earth's atmosphere, beckoning our gaze up.

Question:

What are some of your anchors?

Affirmation:

I am anchored by wonder.

Noticing:

What are you noticing today about what seems barren?

Offering

I am in awe of Carol Ng'ang'a, founder of Msingi Trust, theologian, and justice advocate in Nairobi, Kenya. When the vision of faith we've been handed proves grimy and short-sighted, Ng'ang'a clears the lenses of theology and hope in a single sentence, offering simple and profound words that adjust and realign what we see. As Ng'ang'a and I gathered folks from the African Diaspora to read through Rev. Dr. Randy Woodley's *Becoming Rooted*, she talked about the wonder of the Waorani people of the Amazonian region of Ecuador not naming a tree by its fruit, but instead by how it exists connected to the rest of its ecosystem. This hit me square between the eyes. We can identify and name beings of this Earth solely by what they produce, or we can name them by how they belong.

Question:

What names are you called by that mark your belonging? What names do you use for other beings that mark their belonging?

Affirmation:

I am more than what I can do. First and most, I miraculously *AM* and I belong.

Noticing:

What are you noticing today about belonging and identity?

Offering

Ask yourself: *To whom do I lovingly belong*? Who are the people that you would choose over and over again, and they would choose you right back? Ask yourself: *Where do I feel most myself, most known, most connected*? What creatures and plants and trees and dirt create the landscape of your memories of security, love, and care? You are more than just fruit; more than what you produce. You are a whole part of the whole. Being an image bearer—one who carries the expression of The Eternal with goodness and agency—is the only invitation you need to honor this whole connectedness.

Question:
What illuminates our interconnection most for you?

Affirmation:
I am whole and connected.

Noticing:
What are you noticing today about being chosen?

Offering

Honey, I love a stage. Since I was in my first talent show at four years old, I knew. Throughout childhood, the stage was a place for play, curiosity, and connection. But 35 years after that first encounter, when I'd attempt to take the stage again, I'd have a trauma response to not feeling like I belonged, that familiar sense that I wasn't enough. In a dream, I'd be sitting with a beloved drama teacher from high school (who has since passed) who was giggling at me and a friend. A fellow high school thespian would interpret the dream as my late teacher telling me to chill out and have fun. A current theatre teacher, the very-much-alive Rhyn Clark, would invite me into play and connection. And it would all circle back to the repairing of my broken sense of dignity, my wounded enoughness, my questioned worthiness.

Question:

What have you always loved?

Affirmation:

I am designed for play, curiosity, and connection.

Noticing:

What are you noticing today that is repairing your wonder?

Offering

Drop every extra weight. Let us drop every weight that tells us that misery is all there is. Let us drop every weight that would claim awe as frivolous. Let us drop every weight that deems storytelling for children only, instead of seeing story intrinsically tied up with our place in the cosmos. Drop every weight that names you unworthy instead of calling you wonder-full. Pick up the weight of wonder when you breathe life-giving air that is made life-giving by the trees that were made with the elements of stardust. You are made of that same stardust blown off by a young blue star that lived, got old, and died. Drop every weight that says you don't belong here, in this moment, as your whole self. *You do.*

Question:

What is weighing down your access to wonder?

Affirmation:

I am made of stardust and I belong here.

Noticing:

What are you noticing today about your connection to more-than-human beings?

Offering

To the Earth: thank you. Thank you for every slithery earthworm. Thank you for the peach seed I planted but never grew (I checked all the time... for years!). Thank you for the rain—it is one of my favorite ways to be with you. Thank you for the wild blueberries and cherry tomatoes plucked off the branch. Thank you for the awkward beauty of brussel sprouts and broccoli. Thank you for the sunflowers and lavender, the way the water meets the shore, and the way the trees are the breath of our life. I could thank you for 10,000 years, and it still wouldn't be enough.

Question:

When was the last time you offered gratitude to the Earth?

Affirmation:

I am grateful for all the ways the Earth supports me.

Noticing:

What are you noticing today that didn't turn out the way you wanted, and you are grateful for it anyway?

Offering

Each of the 100 million black holes in the Milky Way has its own horizon and story. Both story and horizons are rooted in perspective and experience. Ultimately, how we create our stories and see the horizon is fundamentally about our location. Our space-time location in the universe does more than just make our planet habitable; it inspires commonalities and narratives among us. This storying is where our experience meets our imagination. What we see *at* the horizon and wonder about *over* the horizon creates a connection between what's in us and what is beyond us.

Question:
What location most influences the stories you tell?

Affirmation:
I am connected to the shared narrative of the collective.

Noticing:
What are you noticing today about the stories of those that are different from you?

"I guess that's very much how our bodies carry memory forward, through DNA and more. We can learn and unlearn a lot of it. We can heal and experience life in many different ways."

Ethel Tawe
BOMB Magazine Interview

Offering

The ubiquitous question "What do you do?" is so tired, as if that is the most important thing about someone. I admit, sometimes that's the *easiest* thing to ask first. But to identify a person—or the Earth—simply by what is produced flattens both the human and the Earth into a vessel for extraction and exploitation. But we —and the Earth—with our beautiful contours could never be flat. Just as the Earth dances in our solar system, you dance with those in your own concentric circles. With wholeness, you exist in a reality of belonging that is far more wonder-full than the separating out of your parts.

Question:

When someone is getting to know you, what would you like to be asked instead of "What do you do?"

Affirmation:

I am full. I am contoured. I am whole.

Noticing:

What are you noticing today about wholeness and connection?

Offering

I am *whole*. And I am *becoming* whole. I think this is the poetry Aomawa Shields, PhD is talking about in her book *Life On Other Planets*. At least, that's the poetry I heard when I read it. The cadence of a complete life, a life that isn't flat or singular but is multi-dimensional and multi-versioned. And somehow, for some reason, it's embodied right here in me, between my lips and the foreheads of my children. Between the laughter shared with my friends. Between my tears and the words I share with my classmates. Layers of an 8-slice pie, crust golden, and berries hot, soft, and sweet. This is me. I *am* the poem.

Question:
When was the last time you read poetry, and what was it?

Affirmation:
I am the poem.

Noticing:
What are you noticing today that makes life feel full, layered, and sweet?

Offering

Do you remember... playing? I know, that's a weird question. I remember. I also remember the wonder that was often associated with play. Running outside, pretending, creating unto discovery and joy. Why did we stop playing? Why did wonder become something rare instead of being the stuff our moments are made of, the fabric of reality? When did we stop dancing to the rhythm of awe? And *why*?

Question:

What is play for you right now, and how does it make you feel?

Affirmation:

I am worthy of wondrous play.

Noticing:

What are you noticing today as you consider the playful elements of living?

Offering

What is visible to the human eye only covers about .0035% of ALL types of light—also known as electromagnetic waves—which come in various lengths. Even if there are wavelengths of luminosity present, if they aren't in the length of visible light, it is darkness to us. Years ago, I was reading Psalm 139 of The Holy Bible A LOT trying to soothe my soul. Unfortunately, it wasn't very comforting. Here's a reference line: "[Eternal One,] You can see in the dark, for it is not dark to your eyes."[37] In my weariness, Psalm 139 offered a God who can see everything and know my thoughts, who I also cannot hide from. *No thanks.* Cause when God is a cosmic Santa Claus with a punitive, auto-updating naughty list, you pray to the light spectrum that you can hide in the valley of a deep wavelength. But listen… if Creator thought you up and excitedly gave you breath and light, Love and life… if *delight* is the very fiber of the cord tethering The Eternal to you… then you get to be all wonder and gratitude at the thought that God *always* sees you. Being seen—truly seen—is only comforting when The Eternal One, seeing you fully illuminated even when you try to hide in the dark, persistently calls you Beloved.

Question:

When are you the most comfortable being fully seen?

Affirmation:

I am luminous in the dark.

Noticing:

What are you noticing today about your relationship to delight?

Offering

The alchemy of humility lies in transforming what is dead into a rich, conditioning composite for our soul-soil. So what happens when things die but they don't fully decay? Can there be a mummification of contracted ways of being? Rather than letting what has become fruitless break down so it becomes useful, life-giving, and alchemized into something rich and nourishing, mummified ways of being become asphyxiating nostalgia. *No life, no air, no transformation*—and every memory is tethered to something dead. If you need it, take this as permission to let it die—whatever "it" is that has convinced you it's holding your hand when its fingers are wrapped around your neck. You can engage in the process by trusting the promise that nothing is wasted, that the seasons still cycle, and that there is hope for life-giving growth after death.

Question:
Where do you need permission to let "it" die?

Affirmation:
I am the alchemist of my own experiences, and alchemy takes time.

Noticing:
What are you noticing today about the wonder in letting things die and transform?

Offering

When nebulae and stars, planets and solar systems die, it feels very *out there*. We haven't experienced the catastrophic results of these deaths simply because we haven't been close enough when they happen. But we've been plenty close when the death of large bushes and trees, family members and loved ones, or promises and hopes comes to sit with us. Those can often feel too close. Some of us go to the garden and put hands in the dirt to ground ourselves, to surround a bleeding heart with life. But it all feels utterly catastrophic. If a gardener is one who tends to life, they also have to be one who tends to death. And you don't just tend to it. Death is something you have to sit with as well. Death takes a seat, pulls one up for you, and you commune at the table of grief. And sometimes that table is set in, however oddly, a garden.

Question:

When death comes, what do you need?

Affirmation:

I am willing to stay close, even when death comes.

Noticing:

What are you noticing today about cycles in the more-than-human world?

Offering

Often, the journey to humility—a grounded, whole expression of self and reciprocity—requires death. And it's not like death happens; you have a funeral; and humility is served at the repass. There has to be death *and* decay for humility to form. My sense of wholeness was preceded by the death of many things that were, at the time, informing my and some of my community's ways of being. One death that stands out to me starkly is that of *Certainty*. Certainty said it addressed my fears, but it just lied about them. Certainty said it was keeping me honest, but it was torturing me with self-hatred. Certainty, among other ways of being, had to be killed, buried, and allowed to decay so my soul-soil could be enriched unto wholeness.

Question:

What has preceded your experiences of your wholeness?

Affirmation:

I am whole and can live from my wholeness.

Noticing:

What are you noticing today that you need to let die so you have a clearer path toward wholeness?

"Before science, humans were making sense of awe in forms of culture."

Dacher Keltner
Awe: The New Science of Everyday Wonder and How It Can Transform Your Life

Offering

I consider myself in the business of bringing cosmic truths down to Earth. Taking what's grand and finding ourselves in it, or finding what's grand inside of us. When cosmic truths come to Earth, they are no longer out there somewhere; they are right here. Celestial awe can be found in the dirt between your fingers and toes. Expansive wonder can be encapsulated in a puffy dandelion. Your tears can hold generations of story, and our connection to one another can tether us to ancient galactic light. How? Distilled all the way down, I really think it's about imagination. Every heart breaks at some point—usually at many points. Sometimes the breaking creates a pile of pieces with hope buried under it. And sometimes... sometimes a heart cracks open and its capacity expands. Either way, imagination is like the gold in the Japanese technique of Kintsugi[38] where broken ceramic is repaired with a golden epoxy, helping our hearts hold the massive weight of cosmic and Earthy wonder.

Question:

What fracture lines on your broken heart have been filled with the golden glue of imagination?

Affirmation:

I am knit together with wonder.

Noticing:

What are you noticing today that breaks in order to expand?

Offering

I'm fascinated by black holes. There are 100 million just in our galaxy, the Milky Way, alone. Did you know each one has a horizon? It's a special kind called an *event horizon*, defined by Wikipedia as "a boundary beyond which events cannot affect an observer." The potential rabbit hole we could dive into head-first is tempting, but I also want to bring up *story* as we consider horizons. A story, as defined by Merriam-Webster, is "an account of incidents or events." We've all heard the accounts that *try* to be event horizons—cutting off observers from what's going on beyond the poorly-created boundary. The problem is that we are far too connected to be unaffected by one another, especially regarding the stories we tell. May we have horizons and stories that don't cut loose but tether us together in community.

Question:

What stories do you tell that tether us to one another?

Affirmation:

I am affected by what I observe because we are inherently connected.

Noticing:

What are you noticing today about where you've created boundaries that are like event horizons?

Offering

Many of us have compared ourselves or others to an onion. You, The Onion, are multi-layered. Your layers hold stories, mark your development, and make up a full and complex expression of who you are. If we pull back every layer of story, every season of growth, we find it is all constructed around the solid core of dignity—your intrinsic worthiness. The center has to be there. It's the foundation the layers grow around. No center, no onion.

Question:

What stories are closest to your center, your dignity?

Affirmation:

I am inherently layered and intrinsically worthy.

Noticing:

What are you noticing today about your trust in your own dignity?

Offering

There are many ways we can give meaning to the dark. Let's look at darkness as necessary, as part of the whole, and not an enemy. In reconsidering darkness, I'm compelled to ask about the darkness within you. You may recoil at the suggestion that there is darkness in you. But remember, we are talking about darkness as a beautiful and necessary part of the greater living whole. Darkness provides space for energy to become life, working in tandem *with* the light, not as the antithesis of it.

Question:

Can you name your beautiful darkness?

Affirmation:

I am luminous and contain the sisters Dark and Light.

Noticing:

What are you noticing about darkness being a partner with light?

Offering

An invocation of your imagination: Imagine humility being of the Earth, being known by your Earth, and embracing the Earthiness of every being. Imagine humility not being a shrinking but an expanding. Imagine humility not being a cutting-off but a rooting down. Imagine humility being like humus: the nutrient-dense, soft, dark, spongy material of your soul. Imagine humility as permission to remove what others have dressed you in that was never yours to wear. Imagine humility as the way to truth and life. Imagine humility as a quality in you that recognizes itself in others and calls them to play in the freedom, warmth, and embrace of abundance. Imagine humility alive in you. Imagine humility not being the one who says, "No, you can't," but what helps you lay hold of the great "I CAN." Imagine humility being individual and collective.

Question:

When you permit yourself to reimagine humility, what happens in your mind? In your body? In your emotions?

Affirmation:

I am humble, grounded, and abundant.

Noticing:

What are you noticing today about where you can identify humility?

Offering

Let me tell it, and my first encounter with wonder in theology was the concept of Imago Dei, The Divine Image. Simplified and in my own words, Imago Dei is the expression of The Eternal in you. Much like Ubuntu—the Bantu word that is often understood, at least in part, as "I am because we/you are"[39]—Imago Dei is inextricably communal. A primary function of Imago Dei, I believe, is naming the goodness of the community of creation in whole, in its parts, and in its interconnectedness. We don't connect fully to our Imago Dei without naming other beings of creation inherently "good." But here's the rub: we aren't adept at even naming our*selves* good, let alone other people or beings. There are so many reasons why, and so I counter every reason with wonder. It is *good* to find the wonder in yourself and live from that place. It is *good* to freely name the wonder in what is around you—oxygen-giving trees growing and flourishing, birds flying and eating together, the human across from you smiling. Wonder and goodness are linked, so whether or not you can get into the Imago Dei concept, you can welcome in the wonder and goodness that is inherently *yours* because it's inherently *ours*.

Question:
What keeps you from trusting your own wonder and goodness?

Affirmation:
I am wonder-full because we are wonder-full.

Noticing:
What are you noticing today that strengthens your connections?

Offering

I learned from two beautiful friends—Karla Mendoza and Samantha E. Lioi—the wonder of a blessing. I received from my mother, Sharon Jacobs, the wonder of a name. I learned from others along my path the wonder of being known, named, and blessed according to where the journey has shaped you, what the relationships forged, and how you are more yourself on the other side of a season. In honor of all this: May you have people who Love you and know your names. May you have people who call you how you've been known. May you feel deep, affirming, textured connection to every name you are given in truth and in Love. And may you always, always, always be known and remembered with wonder.

Question:

What does being "known and remembered with wonder" mean to you?

Affirmation:

I am named Wonder.

Noticing:

What are you noticing today about the wonder that originates in you?

Epilogue

Instead of marveling at the tree, we make plans for its utility. We are a people much more concerned with ruling than loving. This is a mistake that positions us in places where we are no longer close enough to another person or thing to perceive its pain or need. To be human in an aching world is to know our dignity and become people who safeguard the dignity of everything around us.

Cole Arthur Riley
This Here Flesh

There is another kind of wonder not captured in this book. A kind of awe you can find Dacher Keltner and others speaking of as they cover the vast meaning and experience of awe and wonder. It's the kind of wonder we hold in horror of what humanity is capable of doing. The kind of awe that makes us sick to our stomach realizing how deeply disconnected and violent we can be.

I'm writing this at a time where militarized powers—both global and local—are supporting one another in ethnic cleansing and genocide of those they've dehumanized while also terrorizing and even killing their own citizens. Black, Queer, and Indigenous lives, joy, flourishing, and agency not only don't matter, they are all being attacked systemically and systematically. Forced starvation, displacement, war crimes, and trauma on civilians are actively going on across our shared blue dot.

Ecologically, the crisis we have created and continue to perpetuate has already deeply damaged the only place in the universe we call home—at a rate that leaves us unsure if the effects are reversible. There is intentional erasure of histories and identities, regularly there are sacrifices of our interpersonal flourishing on the altar of being right, and a loneliness epidemic is the subject of many reports around widespread well-being.

Wonder isn't the golden ticket to fix these issues.

But.

Wonder does stretch our imagination toward an existence of collective flourishing.

Wonder reminds us that it doesn't have to be this way. Wonder gives us something bigger than what's right in front of us to look to, to engage with, and to stretch what we believe is possible. The kind of wonder that whispers to us from the stars and is offered to us by the trees and twinkles in the eyes of every beloved can make us pause from what Rowan White calls "cultural insanity"[40] and look up. Or look down. Or put our hands in the dirt. Or weep at how distant we've gotten from wonder and what we've filled that distance with—destructive, utterly harmful ways of being with ourselves, one another, and our fellow more-than-human beings.

What can we do? We can pause. We can be honest about our own suffering, and stay open to those suffering right in front of us, across the room, or across land or waters, and then...fill the space with what awe offers. Listening. Action. Care. Learning. Joy.

I do not believe wonder can be decimated. I know our *hope* can be, especially when we've seen and been through the worst humanity has to offer. Our imagination becomes frozen from the realities we experience and bear witness to. And yet, wonder remains. Wonder is a flame of fire, thawing out what we are able to believe is possible. Wonder is a core ingredient in the brothy soup humanity needs to eat to heal. Wonder reminds us that there is, and has always been, another awe-worn way. And, friend, I think this is our way home.

People need to know that we live in a universe that is bigger than the bad things that are happening to us.[41]

Margaret Prescod
Activist, Author, Journalist, and Radio Host

Footnotes

1. Deidra Riggs is a professional JEDI Coach, anti-racist educator, author, and speaker. You can find out more about her at https://deidrariggs.com

2. https://science.nasa.gov/universe/overview/building-blocks#hds-sidebar-nav-3

3. https://www.energy.gov/nnsa/articles/visible-light-eye-opening-research-nnsa#:~:text=The%20entire%20rainbow%20of%20radiation,electromagnetic%20spectrum%20%E2%80%93%20about%200.0035%20percent.

4. https://www.who.int/news-room/questions-and-answers/item/radiation-the-known-health-effects-of-ultraviolet-radiation

5. https://en.wikipedia.org/wiki/Quasar

6. https://en.wikipedia.org/wiki/Ubuntu_philosophy . Additional translation information can be found at https://iep.utm.edu/hunhu-ubuntu-southern-african-thought/#H3

7. https://www.ted.com/talks/shonda_rhimes_my_year_of_saying_yes_to_eve rything?language=en

8. You can find all the scientific information for this entry in various places, including Carl Sagan's book *Cosmos* (I highly recommend the audiobook—THE Levar Burton reads it), and in this NASA article with a simplified version of the information: https://astrobiology.nasa.gov/education/alp/are-we-really-made-of-star-stuff/#:~:text=Then%2C%20later%20on%2C%20when%20new,are%20made%20of%20star%20stuff!

9. https://www.theatlantic.com/science/archive/2023/06/universe-gravitational-waves-nanograv-discovery/674570/

10. https://earthsky.org/astronomy-essentials/definition-what-is-a-neutron-star/ ; Gater, W. (2020). The Mysteries of the Universe (DK Children's Anthologies). DK Children.

11. https://www.instagram.com/blackcoffeewithwhitefriends/

12. Carl Sagan is quoted saying, "We are made of star-stuff. We are a way for the universe to know itself" during the 1980 mini-series *Cosmos* which he hosted. https://www.imdb.com/title/tt0081846/characters/nm0755981

13. https://science.nasa.gov/solar-system/

14. https://en.wikipedia.org/wiki/Galaxy#:~:text=It%20is%20estimated%20that%20there,of%20parsecs%20(or%20megaparsecs)

15. Gater, W. (2020). *The Mysteries of the Universe* (DK Children's Anthologies). DK Children

116.
https://www.stsci.edu/~marel/black_holes/encyc_mod3_q7.html#:~:text=
T
he%20Milky%20Way%20galaxy%20contains,million%20stellar%2Dmass%2
0black%20holes.

17. This is a fun, contextual term I'm using here to refer to The Eternal.

18. DK. (2020). *Universe*, Third Edition (DK Definitive Visual Encyclopedias),
p 238

19. https://www.nasa.gov/image-article/butterfly-nebula-2/

20. Gater, W. (2020). *The Mysteries of the Universe* (DK Children's
Anthologies). DK Children.

21. Shklovskii, I.S. and Sagan, C. (1998). *Intelligent Life in the Universe*.
Emerson Adams Pr Inc

22. Sagan, C. (1980). *Cosmos* (1st ed.). Random House.

23. I don't have a singular source to cite here, as the synthesizing has
happened over years of time and input from a variety of beings, places,
and experiences. Influences like The Eternal themselves, my intuition,
creation stories in the Genesis book of The Holy Bible and Rev. Dr. Wilda
Gafney's ancient Hebrew linguistic clarity in her book, *Womanist Midrash*
regarding them. Also, many episodes of *How The Universe Works*, books like
The Mysteries of the Universe by Will Gater, Aramaic translations by Neil
Douglas-Klotz, and hours of exchange with my broad spiritual community,
are just some.

24. I learned about this primordial essentiality of hydrogen in season 11, episode 3 of *How The Universe Works*, currently streaming on Discovery+.

25. Woodley, R. *Becoming Rooted: 100 Days of Reconnecting with Sacred Earth*. 2022. Broadleaf Books.

26. Keltner speaks on this extensively with beautiful examples in his book *Awe* in chapter five which is titled "Collective Effervescence". Keltner, D. *Awe: The New Science of Everyday Wonder and How It Can Transform Your Life*. 2023. Penguin Books.

27. https://en.wikipedia.org/wiki/Leontopodium_nivale

28. Please go listen to Leslie Odom, Jr. and Nicolette Robinson sing their version of "Edelweiss" from *The Sound of Music* soundtrack

9. If you are interested in creation and cosmology stories, a book I've learned from is *Creation Stories: Landscapes and the Human Imagination* by Anthony Aveni.

30. https://en.wikipedia.org/wiki/Leontopodium_nivale

31. Aki, A. (2023). *Joie: A Parisian's Guide to Celebrating the Good Life*. Clarkson Potter.

32. Dr. Khanyezi has her Ph.D in Healing Racial Trauma from Howard university and is a certified somatics practitioner. You can find out more about her work at gigionline.org.

33. https://www.findingourwaypodcast.com/individual-episodes/s2e6

34. You can read more and find addition sources at
https://hikersnotebook.blog/fauna/butterflies-moths-and-caterpillars/red-spotted-purple-butterfly/

35. Bebo Norman. (2004). "Borrow Mine" [song]. On Try. Essential Records.

36 Shields PhD, A. *Life On Other Planets: A Memoir of Finding My Place in the Universe*. Viking.

37. *The Voice Translation Bible*, 2012, Ps. 139:12

38. You can learn more about this art form at
https://en.wikipedia.org/wiki/Kintsugi

39. https://www.africaw.com/african-philosophy-ubuntu-a-way-of-life;
https://en.wikipedia.org/wiki/Ubuntu

40. https://www.findingourwaypodcast.com/individual-episodes/s2e6

41. This quote is from a conversation shared in *The Disordered Cosmos* between the author, Chanda Prescod-Weinstein and Margaret Prescod, the author's mother.

Author's Bio

Hi! I'm Nya and thank you for reading my book (and the author's page, wow!). I am a world builder. An intuitive and empath who is also an astronomy and human behavior nerd, I feel and care deeply about many people, places, and things—and the connection of it all. It's from this place that I seek to wildly follow my curiosity about the internal and relational worlds we can build on the foundations of Dignity & Wonder.

I speak and facilitate at my company, The Dignity Effect. I write and talk about wonder and awe in my digital publication *Of Earth & Of Stars*. Increasingly, I find it hard to separate the two. You'll find dignity and wonder woven into both of my vocational expressions.

I was raised and currently live on the ancestral lands of the Mvskoke (Muscogee) and Tsalaguwetiyi (Cherokee, East) peoples. Many of their descendants are not currently living in this place. I honor the Mvskoke and Tsalaguwetiyi, the original stewards and Beloveds of these lands.

The folks who have supported and endured the birthing of this book day in and day out include my husband Myron, my kids Phoenix and Justice, and the broad, beautiful community that keeps and Loves us so well.